Mr. Wiggle's Library

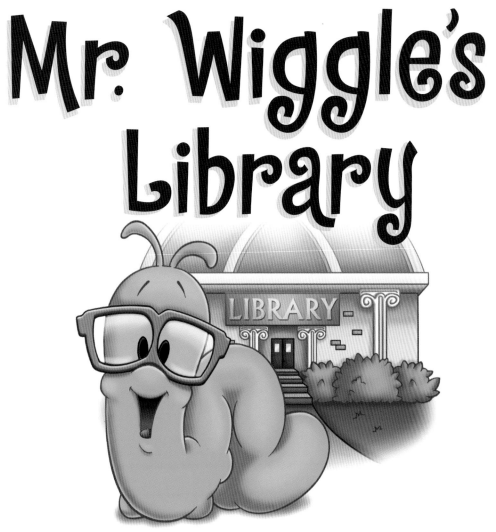

By Carol Thompson
Illustrated by Bobbie Houser

 School Specialty
Publishing

Columbus, Ohio

This product has been aligned to state and national content standards to facilitate the evaluation and improvement of academic standards and student achievement. To find how this product aligns to your standards, go to www.SchoolSpecialtyPublishing.com.

Copyright © 2004 School Specialty Publishing, a member of the School Specialty Family.

Printed in the United States of America. All rights reserved. Except as permitted under the United States Copyright Act, no part of this publication may be reproduced or distributed in any form or by any means, or stored in a database or retrieval system, without prior written permission from the publisher, unless otherwise indicated.

Library of Congress Cataloging-in-Publication Data is on file with the publisher.

Send all inquiries to:
School Specialty Publishing
8720 Orion Place
Columbus, OH 43240-2111

ISBN 1-57768-613-6

3 4 5 6 7 8 PHX 11 10 09 08 07 06

Hello. My name is Mr. Wiggle,
And there's a smile upon my face.
Because today I went to visit
The most interesting place.

I traveled to the library.
You'll never guess what I saw.
Lots of books and other neat things,
I was totally in awe!

LIBRARIAN

Someone was there to help me
And show me all around.
I couldn't believe my own worm eyes
What a great place I had found!

She said:

"Right when you walk in the door,
There's a drop box marked *Returns*."
This is where I put my books
When I'm finished with them, I learned.

"There is also a special area
For books that are easier to read.
Until you get a little older,
This is probably what you'll need."

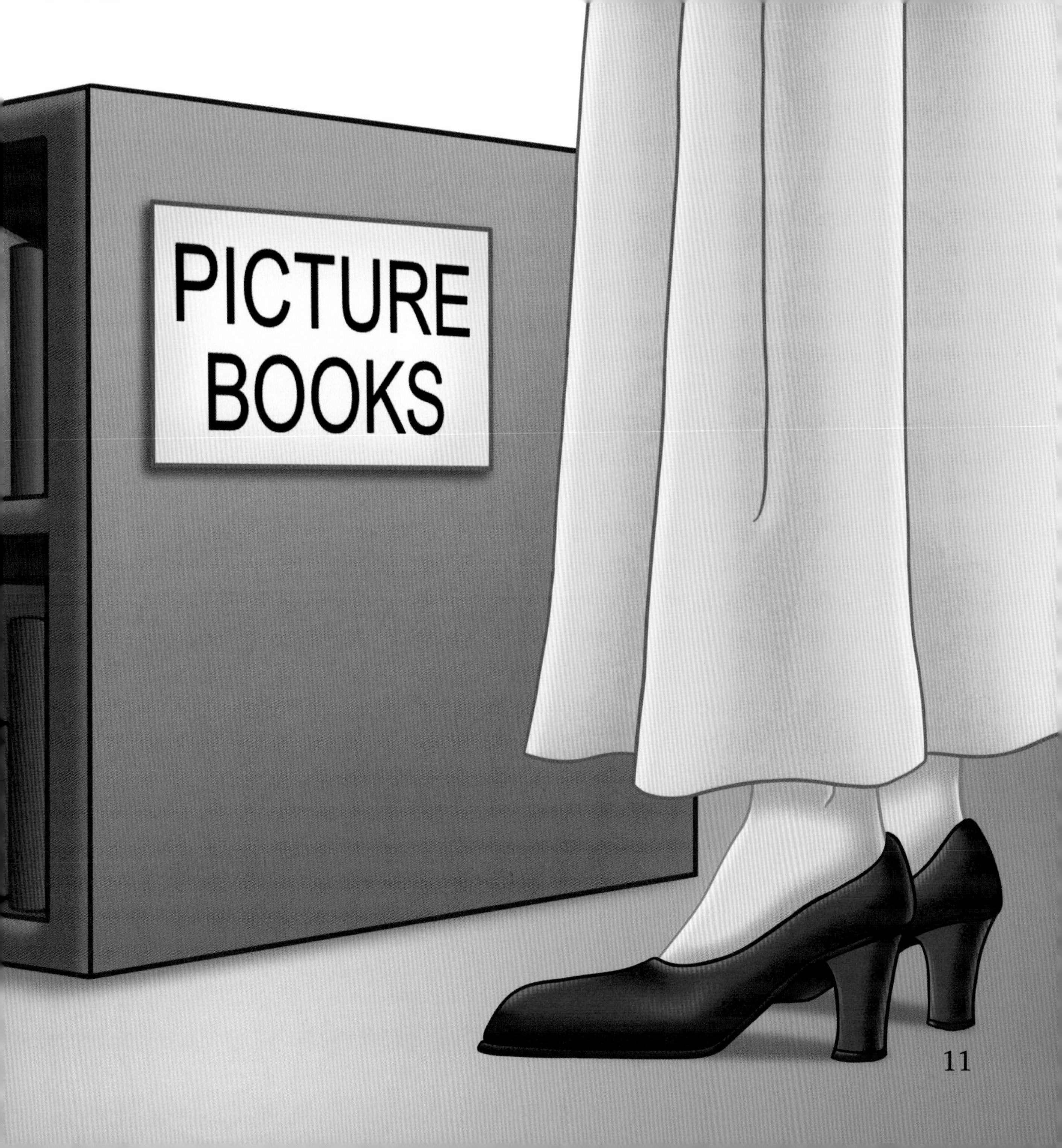
PICTURE
BOOKS

"The nonfiction books are over here,
Just walk in this direction.
Poetry, fact, and true-life books
Are all in this collection."

"There also is a special display
For books that have won awards.
Pick a Newbery or a Caldecott
And, trust me, you won't be bored!"

WORLD NEWS

THE REFLECTOR

SPORTS

RTAIN

"Newspapers are on a special rack.
You can sit down here and read
Today's events, weather, or sports.
You'll enjoy it, guaranteed!"

17

"Library computers are often used
For a variety of jobs.
Like surfing the Web, typing a paper,
Or searching the card catalog."

18

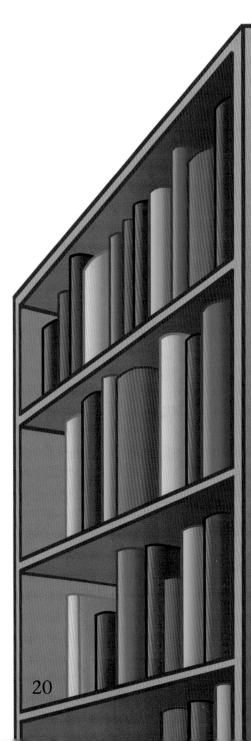

"Over there is yet another section—
The one that's called *Reference*.
When you've got a hard research topic,
This section will help it make sense."

20

"In this section, you'll find reference tools
Like an atlas or dictionary.
You can use them while you're studying.
They're really quite extraordinary."

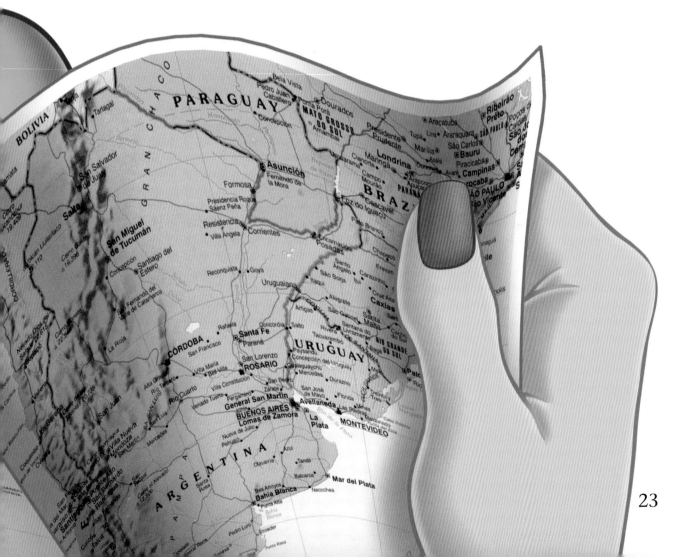

"You may like to read magazines
And think they're pretty cool.
They are full of current information
That can help you out at school."

"One last little bit of information,
This rule is important, second to none.
Make sure when you're at the library
That you have lots and lots of fun!"

"Thank you, Ms. Librarian,
For taking me on a tour.
I can't wait to get started,
I'll find lots to read, I'm sure!"

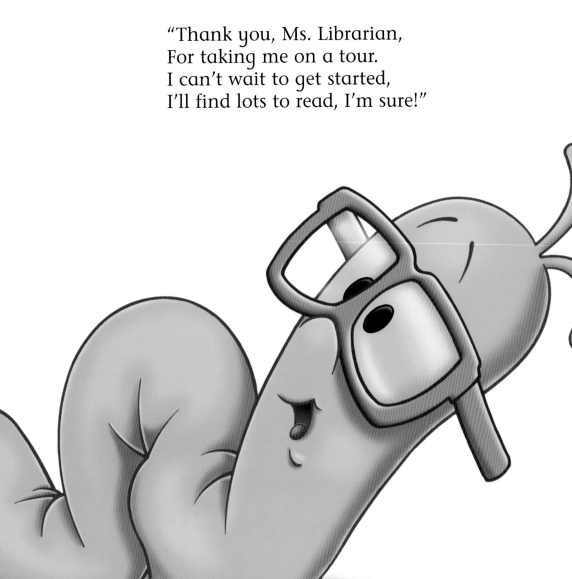

"I was happy to show you around.
It wasn't even hard.
Just remember, little worm,
Don't lose your library card!"

This Library Card
Belongs to

Mr. Wiggle

31

My name is Mr. Wiggle.
I am a library bookworm.
I visited the library today,
So now it is *your* turn!

KINGSTON UPON THAMES PUBLIC LIBRARIES

On line Services

Royal Kingston

www.kingston.gov.uk/libraries

Renew a book (3 times)   Request a book
Change of address   Email a branch
Library news and updates   Get your pin
Search the catalogues   Access free reference sites

020 854_____6

KT-416-415

2 1 MAR 2013	1 7 AUG 2013	
1 8 MAY 2013		
2 4 JUN 2013	2 7 AUG 2013	
	0 SEP 2013	
	0 4 APR 2016	
	0 7 MAR 2017	

1 1 MAY 2012

KT 0789993 9

First published 2004 by Walker Books Ltd
87 Vauxhall Walk, London SE11 5HJ

This edition published 2006

10 9 8 7 6 5 4 3 2 1

Text © 2004 Vivian French

Illustrations © 2004 Alison Bartlett

The right of Vivian French and Alison Bartlett to be
identified as author and illustrator respectively of this work
has been asserted by them in accordance with the
Copyright, Designs and Patents Act 1988

This book has been typeset in Journal
and Tree-Boxelder

Printed in China

All rights reserved. No part of this book may be reproduced,
transmitted or stored in an information retrieval system
in any form or by any means, graphic, electronic
or mechanical, including photocopying, taping
and recording, without prior written
permission from the publisher.

British Library Cataloguing in Publication Data:
a catalogue record for this book is
available from the British Library

ISBN 13: 978-1-4063-0170-0
ISBN 10: 1-4063-0170-1

www.walkerbooks.co.uk

KINGSTON UPON THAMES
PUBLIC LIBRARIES

0 7 8 99 939

ALL	CLASS	
NM	JNF	
CAT	REF	
5.99	07/07	

For John Joe
V. F.

For Lucie, Steve,
Oscar and
Harry - much love
A. B.

T. REX

VIVIAN FRENCH

illustrated by

ALISON BARTLETT

THIS WAY FOR THE
T. REX EXHIBITION

WALKER BOOKS
AND SUBSIDIARIES

LONDON · BOSTON · SYDNEY · AUCKLAND

It began with an egg!

What size was
the egg?

The egg was as big as your head ... perhaps.

Don't you know? Why don't you know?

Lots of dinosaur fossil egg shells have been found, but nobody knows if any of them belong to Tyrannosaurus rex. (Fossils are the remains of animals or plants that lived long ago.)

It was millions and millions of years ago!

Was the egg in a nest?

Was the nest in a tree?

8

The egg was buried in sand ...
perhaps.

The way fossil egg shells lie suggests they have been resting on a sandy base.

Don't you know? Why don't you know?
It was millions and millions of years ago!

And the sun beamed down, and the sand grew hot. And the egg cracked open, and what came out? A tiny dinosaur. A carnosaur. Tyrannosaur – TYRANNOSAURUS REX!

Carnosaur means meat-eater.
Tyrannosaur means tyrant lizard.
Rex means king.

And how did he grow?
Or don't you know?

It was millions and
millions of years ago!

There was danger there. Wherever he went
were carnosaurs – the eaters of meat –
walking and stalking and sniffing about.

ADULT GORGOSAURUS

ADULT ALBERTOSAURUS

There were lots of big meat-eating dinosaurs,
including Gorgosaurus and Albertosaurus.

Young dinosaurs would have had to watch out.

An adult Tyrannosaurus rex was twelve metres long and five to six metres high.

And anything moving might have been LUNCH! Munch! Crunch!

ADULT T. REX

It weighed over seven tonnes.

Females were bigger than males.

13

But he ducked and
he dived and he ate
and he grew.

With his two strong legs
and dagger-clawed toes,

No one knows what kind of noise
Tyrannosaurus rex might have made.

14

and his scaly skin and his hungry
eyes and his terrible teeth...

Small pieces of fossilized skin have been found, but
we have no idea what colour dinosaurs really were.

15

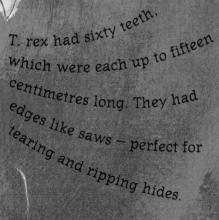

T. rex had sixty teeth, which were each up to fifteen centimetres long. They had edges like saws — perfect for tearing and ripping hides.

How were his teeth, his terrible teeth?
Were they sharp? Were they long?
Were they terribly strong?

Did he rip and tear as he charged and leapt,
as he thundered after his panicking prey?

Maybe yes,
or maybe no –
it was millions and millions of years ago.

He MIGHT have leapt and lunged and ripped,
or he MIGHT have wandered for miles and miles,
sniffing the air for the smell of flesh,
flesh that was dying or flesh that was dead –
he might have hunted for secondhand prey,
a scavenger clearing
the dead away.

The fossil skulls of carnosaurs like T. rex show they had
very sensitive nostrils and a good sense of smell.

Did he hunt with his friends?
Did he hunt with his mate?

No one knows how fast Tyrannosaurus rex would
have moved. Scientists sometimes guess from
tracks, but only a single tyrannosaur
fossil footprint has been found. (So far.)

Tyrannosaurus rex skeletons

are usually found on their own.

He probably hunted and ate alone,
but then again – we don't really know.

It was millions and millions of years ago...

You keep saying that, but I want to know –
how can I know what's REALLY true?

22

The answer is that it's up to you –
you can look at those dinosaur bones.

Now, do YOU think he walked or ran?
How do you think he found his food?

Did he roar? Did he growl?
Did he rumble and purr?

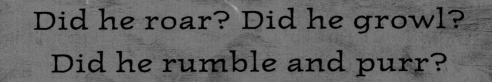

How did he live and
how did he
die?

Did he care for his babies
or leave them
alone?

Maybe one day we'll REALLY know...
Maybe we'll know what's really true.

There is so much we don't know about dinosaurs yet: only more discoveries will help us to find the answers. Scientists who study dinosaurs are called palaeontologists. (Will that be you?)

The person to tell us
might just be YOU!

Index

Look up the pages to find out about all these T. rex things. Don't forget to look at all the kinds of words – **this kind**, *this kind* and this kind.

28

ABOUT THE AUTHOR

Vivian French lives in Edinburgh and has written dozens of books. "I've always loved dinosaurs," *she says,* "and T. rex in particular – it's the SIZE! The fact we know so little about them fascinates me. In my lifetime the experts have changed their minds many times over. Maybe T. rex will turn out to be a dragon!"

ABOUT THE ILLUSTRATOR

Alison Bartlett lives in Bath with her son, Joel. Together they have searched for dinosaur fossils but are yet to find one. Instead, they regularly make dinosaur models, and have even built a dinosaur land, with the help of Emma, their neighbour.

ABOUT THE T. REX

The only thing we know for sure about Tyrannosaurus rex is that it was a big dinosaur that lived 65–85 million years ago. The rest is just guessing. That's what is so exciting. Someone might discover something next week, next year or in twenty years' time that tells us a whole lot more. And who knows ... it might just be you!

NOTES FOR TEACHERS

The READ AND WONDER series is an innovative and versatile resource for reading, thinking and discovery. Each book invites children to become excited about a topic, see how varied information books can be, and want to find out more.

Reading aloud The story form makes these books ideal for reading aloud – in their own right or as part of a cross-curricular topic, to a child or to a whole class. After you've introduced children to the books in this way, they can revisit and enjoy them again and again.

Shared reading Big Book editions are available for several titles, so children can read along, discuss the topic, and comment on the different ways information is presented – to wonder together.

Group and guided reading Children need to experience a range of reading materials. Information books like these help develop the skills of reading to learn, as part of learning to read. With the support of a reading group, children can become confident, flexible readers.

Paired reading It's fun to take turns to read the information in the main text or in the captions. With a partner, children can explore the pages to satisfy their curiosity and build their understanding.

Individual reading These books can be read for interest and pleasure by children at home and in school.

Research Once children have been introduced to these books through reading aloud, they can use them for independent or group research, as part of a curricular topic.

Children's own writing You can offer these books as strong models for children's own information writing. They can record their observations and findings about a topic, make field notes and sketches, and add extra snippets of information for the reader.

Above all, Read and Wonders are to be enjoyed, and encourage children to develop a lasting curiosity about the world they live in.

Sue Ellis, Centre for Language in Primary Education

Kingston Libraries

This item can be returned
or renewed at a Kingston
Borough Library on or
before the latest date
stamped below. If the item
is not reserved by another
reader it may be renewed
by telephone up to a
maximum of three times by
quoting your membership
number. Only items issued
for the standard three-week
loan period are renewable.

www.kingston.gov.uk/libraries

Royal
Kingston

New Malden Library
43 Kingston Road
New Malden
KT3   5006
Tel: 8547 6490

23. DEC. 06.	— 014	- 4 OCT 2014
KT-416-418	02 AUG 2011	4/17 7
20. JAN 07		
06. JUL. 07		
23. OCT. 08.	2 2 AUG 2013	
	9/13 2 1	
	- 6 JAN 2014	
14. FEB. 09.	1 9 DEC 2015	
0 5 APR 2011		

INVESTOR IN PEOPLE

KT 0778958 0

Plastic

by Claire Llewellyn

W
FRANKLIN WATTS
LONDON • SYDNEY

KINGSTON UPON THAMES
PUBLIC LIBRARIES

07789580

ALL	CLASS	
NM	J 668	
CAT	REF	
P 5.99	5/06	

This edition 2005
Franklin Watts
96 Leonard Street
London EC2A 4XD

Franklin Watts Australia
Level 17/207 Kent Street
Sydney NSW 2000

Text copyright © Claire Llewellyn 2002

ISBN 0 7496 6373 1

Dewey Decimal
Classification Number: 668.4

A CIP catalogue record for this book is
available from the British Library

Series editor: Rosalind Beckman
Series designer: James Evans
Picture research: Diana Morris
Photography: Steve Shott

Printed in China

Acknowledgements

Thanks are due to the following for kind permission to
reproduce photographs:

James Davis Travel Photography: 16-17b. Julio Etchart/Still
Pictures: 22r. Chris Fairclough/Franklin Watts: 7clb, 8t, 8b.
Peter Frischmuth/Still Pictures: 27t. Pascal Goetgheluck/SPL:
19r. Nick Hanna/Eye Ubiquitous: 1lt. Robert Harding PL: 14-15c.
Images Colour Library: back cover. Helen Lisher/Eye
Ubiquitous: 1lc. Maximillian Stock Ltd/Robert Harding PL: 18b.
Ray Moller/Franklin Watts: 7r, 9t. NASA/SPL: 2lb. Stephen
Rafferty/Eye Ubiquitous: 12l. Skjold/Eye Ubiquitous: 25t. Tek
Image/SPL: 23t.

Thanks are also due to John Lewis and Vita Thermoplastic
Compounds Ltd for their help with this book.

Contents

Words printed in **bold italic** are explained in the glossary.

What is plastic?

Plastic is one of the most useful materials in the world. It is used to make  thousands of different things. Look around and you'll see plastic everywhere - in homes, cars, hospitals and schools. It is hard to imagine life without it.

All sorts of plastic

The name 'plastic' is given to hundreds of very different materials. Some people use the word 'plastics' instead. One kind of plastic often looks and feels different from another, and may behave in different ways.

Made of plastic

All the things in these pictures are made of plastic. Can you name them all?

Material words

Which of these words describe plastic?

cold   thick   shiny

sticky   stretchy

stiff   solid

heavy

soft   strong

dull

hard

warm

hard-wearing

spongy   light

crisp

colourful

rough   smooth

thin

bendy

slimy

springy

runny

squashy

TOMATO SAUCE

Fantastic fact

The word 'plastic' describes materials that can be bent or moulded into shape. Plasticine is one of these.

Plastic can be hard or soft

Plastics are not all the same. Some of them are hard and strong. Others are squashy and soft. We use these different kinds of plastic in very different ways.

Hard plastics

Hard plastic can be shaped to make things like tables and chairs, dustbins and flower pots. This sort of plastic is very sturdy and always keeps its shape.

Garden equipment is often made of plastic. This is because plastic is strong and easy to clean.

Soft plastics

Soft plastic is not as strong as hard plastic and does not keep its shape. It can be rolled or folded up small. This sort of plastic is used to make things like umbrellas and bags.

Try this

All the items in this picture are made of plastic. Some of them are hard. Others are soft. Can you put them in order from the hardest to the softest?

Plastic is light - but strong

Plastic can be very strong. Many strong materials such as concrete or wood are heavy. But plastic isn't heavy; it is very light. This makes it especially useful.

A plastic basket is very light but it can hold a lot of washing.

Easier to carry

Plastic bottles and tubes are used to carry all sorts of goods - from milk and fruit juice, to paint and shampoo. Plastic bottles are lighter than glass. This makes them easier to carry and cheaper to transport.

Plastic bottles are safer than glass. If you drop them, they will not break.

Lighter than before

Aeroplanes and cars were once made of heavy materials such as metal, leather and wood. Now many of the parts are made of plastic instead. As cars and planes are so much lighter, they need less *energy* to move. This means that they burn a lot less fuel.

Inside a plane there are hundreds of different plastic parts.

Plastic parts are used all over a car - even under the bonnet!

Try this

Plastic bags are light but strong. How many potatoes can you put in a bag before the handles stretch? How many can you put in before the handles break?

Plastic is clean and hard-wearing

Plastic is useful in the home. It is easy to care for, lasts a long time and comes in many different colours.

Easy care

Some materials such as wood or metal need a lot of care. They need polishing, painting, cleaning or oiling to keep them looking good. Plastic is much easier to look after. Plastic does not rust or break, and is hard to mark or scratch.

Plastic window frames last longer than wood and do not need to be painted.

Lots of wear

Think of all the household goods that are made of plastic - vacuum cleaners, kettles, worktops, cutting boards, food containers, floorings and kitchen tools. Some of these things are washed every day. They all take very hard wear.

Fantastic fact

False teeth are made of plastic. They are hard-wearing and easy to clean!

Plastic is waterproof

Plastic is a **waterproof** material. It does not let water or other liquids through. Plastic helps to keep things dry and is very useful out of doors.

Keeps out the weather

Plastic is useful for outdoor equipment such as climbing frames, wheelbarrows and pipes. It lasts for many years because it does not rust or rot in wet weather. Plastic can also be made into waterproof cloth, which is great for wet-weather gear. Rain runs off a plastic coat, which helps to keep you dry.

14

Keeps out the wet

Some things spoil if they get wet, especially if they are made of paper. Look at the cover of this book. A thin layer of plastic protects it if it gets wet or needs wiping clean. At markets, plastic sheets provide a 'roof' for stalls to protect goods and shoppers from the rain.

Goods spoil quickly in the rain. A plastic 'roof' helps to protect them.

Try this

Find two pieces of wallpaper – one with a coating of plastic and one without. Each day, mark them with a washable felt pen. When the ink is dry, wipe them clean with a damp cloth. After a week, compare the two. What do you find?

Plastic is made from oil

Plastic is not a **natural** material. It was invented by scientists. It is made from the **chemicals** in oil.

Inventing plastics

Oil is a valuable material that is found deep inside the ground. When the **crude oil** is taken to an **oil refinery**, most of it is used to make fuel. However, some oil is used to make plastic. Scientists are always searching for new materials. By **experimenting** with different chemicals in oil, they have invented many different kinds of plastic.

Plastic is made from oil at huge factories called oil refineries.

16

From oil to granules

Sometimes powdered wood or clay is added to plastic, to make a stronger or smoother material. Adding **dyes** produces plastic in many different colours. Oil refineries produce plastic in tiny **granules** or chips. These are delivered to factories, which then turn them into goods.

At the factory, the fine granules of plastic are made into many different goods.

Fantastic fact

It takes just two handfuls of plastic granules to make a washing-up bowl.

Plastic is easy to shape

At the factory, the plastic is heated until it melts. It can then be shaped by different machines.

Moulding plastic

When the plastic granules are heated, they melt into a treacly *liquid*. The runny plastic is squeezed, pressed or blown into *moulds*, where it quickly cools and hardens. Moulds are used to make all sorts of goods such as plastic bowls and toys.

Melted plastic looks like a thick, gooey syrup.

Squeezing and fizzing

The melted plastic is shaped in other ways, too. Squeezing it through holes produces hollow tubes that can be turned into hoses, pipes and bags. Fizzing gas into the melted plastic fills it with bubbles. This makes a light, very springy foam such as *polystyrene*.

This machine is making plastic bags. A tube of soft plastic is filled with air before it is flattened and cut.

Try this

Examine two different things made of polystyrene. Why is this material so useful?

Plastic can be made into fibres

Soft plastic can be used to make **fibres**. The fibres are **woven** into many kinds of cloth that last well and are easy to care for.

The finest synthetic fibres are made into sewing thread.

Making the fibres

If runny plastic is squirted through tiny holes, it makes long, thin plastic fibres. These harden as they cool, and can be used for weaving or knitting. Scientists have invented dozens of different fibres such as nylon, **polyester**, acrylic and microfibre. These are called **synthetic** fibres.

Polyester can be used to make all these different fabrics.

1 This fabric has the uneven feel of linen.

2 Layers of fine polyester are used for filling quilts, cushions and pillows.

3 This fine polyester has the look and feel of silk.

4 Polyester sparkles when it is woven with metal thread.

5 A shiny, smooth polyester looks like satin.

New materials

Synthetic fibres are used in different ways. Some are good for making carpets and chairs because they are **fireproof** and don't show the dirt. Many other fibres are used to make clothes. Some of them are shiny like silk, or warm and fluffy like wool.

Clothes made from synthetic fabrics are cheap to produce, comfortable to wear and very easy to care for.

Fantastic fact

The flag on the moon is made of nylon. Nylon was the first cloth ever to be made from plastic.

Plastic makes rubbish

Plastic goods are hard to throw away.
They do not rot and cannot be burned safely.
Getting rid of plastic is a serious problem.
It is one we have to try and solve.

Getting rid of plastic

It is hard to get rid of old plastic bottles and bags. Burying plastic waste does not work; it simply stays in the ground. Burning plastic is dangerous. When it burns, it produces **gases** that poison and **pollute** the air. Plastic rubbish is building up and causing problems for the **environment**.

Plastic rubbish looks ugly on the ground and will not rot away.

Too many landfills

In most towns, rubbish is buried in *landfill sites*. These ugly, smelly places produce harmful gases and attract rats and other pests. Plastic rubbish takes up a lot of space. As we throw away more and more plastic, we will need more and more ugly landfill sites. We need to use plastic carefully and cut down on plastic waste.

Landfill sites are one way of getting rid of rubbish, but they harm the environment.

Try this

Find a plastic cup and a paper cup and bury them under the ground. Remember to mark the spot. A few weeks later, dig up the cups and compare them. What do you notice?

23

Cutting down on plastic

As more goods are made out of plastic, more of them end up in the bin. We need to use plastic more carefully, so that there will be less of it to throw away.

Too much plastic

Throwing away plastic is a waste. It is not just a waste of the material itself; it is a waste of the oil and energy that were used to produce it. We need to use plastic more carefully and save it whenever we can.

All plastic food containers end up as litter. Paper bags or boxes would be a better choice

Some towns have plastic banks where waste plastic can be recycled.

Making savings

Saving plastic helps to protect the environment. There are three ways of doing this. We can reduce the amount of plastic we use - for example, by cutting down on packaging. We can re-use some plastic products - for example, by using one good plastic bag instead of dozens of cheaper carriers. And we can **recycle** waste plastic by taking it to the plastic bank so that it can be turned into recycled plastic.

Try this

If you eat a packed lunch, try to re-use the same box and bottle each day, instead of throwing them away when you have finished eating.

Some plastic can be recycled

Some plastic can be recycled and used to make new things. But recycling plastic is not easy. There are many different types of plastic and each one needs to be recycled on its own.

Sorting plastic

Plastic bottles are made of different kinds of plastic. Most of them are now marked with a code to show what kind of plastic it is. This helps people to sort out their bottles ready for recycling. In some places, they can take them to plastic bottle banks.

All these bottles can be recycled and made into new plastic goods.

Recycling plastic

The old plastic is taken to a factory and heated until it melts. It is then made into new things such as flower pots, traffic cones, outdoor furniture and bags. It can also be recycled into polyester fibre, which can be used to make cloth.

Plastic rubbish arrives at the factory for recycling.

Fantastic fact

Each of us throws away about 50 kg of plastic waste every year – that's enough to make 900 bottles.

Glossary

Chemicals	The tiny substances that join together to make a material such as plastic or oil.
Crude oil	The thick, black oil that is found in the ground.
Dye	A strongly coloured substance that is used to add colour to plastic.
Energy	The power that makes machines and living things able to work.
Environment	All the world around us, including the land, the air and the sea.
Experiment	To try out something new.
Fibre	A long, fine thread.
Fireproof	Cannot be damaged by fire.
Gas	A substance that is neither a liquid nor a solid, like air.
Granule	A small grain.
Landfill site	A place where rubbish is buried.
Liquid	A runny substance such as water that has no shape.

Mould	A container with a special shape. Melted plastic can be poured into a mould to take on its shape.
Natural	Found in the world around us.
Oil refinery	A factory where crude oil is made into fuels, plastics and other materials.
Pollute	To spoil or poison the air, land or water with harmful substances.
Polyester	A synthetic material used to make clothes and other things.
Polystyrene	A very light plastic material.
Recycle	To take an object or material and use it to make something else.
Synthetic	Not natural; made by people.
Waterproof	Something that does not let water through.
Weave	Make cloth by passing threads over and under one another.

Index